P9-EFI-454

# HOW TO PEE

## POTTY TRAINING FOR GIRLS

### TODD SPECTOR, M.D.

Illustrated by
### ARREE CHUNG

HENRY HOLT AND COMPANY

NEW YORK

I would like to dedicate this book to my children, Noa and Abe, who bring me happiness every day and inspire me to think like a kid. Thank you, Erica and Amy, for your hard work and diligence putting this book together with me—I would never have done it without you. Thank you, Daleet, for being a loving and supportive wife who reminds me every day what I am capable of. Finally, thank you to my patients from whom I have learned everything about medicine. —T. S.

For Peregryn and Juniper —A. C.

Henry Holt and Company, LLC
*Publishers since 1866*
175 Fifth Avenue
New York, New York 10010
mackids.com

Library of Congress Cataloging-in-Publication Data
Spector, Todd.
How to pee : potty training for girls / Todd Spector ;
illustrated by Arree Chung.—First edition.
pages       cm
Summary: "Making potty training a game instead of a chore,
this time for girls!"—Provided by publisher.
ISBN 978-1-62779-297-4 (hardback)
1. Toilet training—Juvenile literature. 2. Urination—Juvenile literature.
3. Girls—Health and hygiene—Juvenile literature.  I. Chung, Arree, illustrator. II. Title.
HQ770.5.S693 2015       649'.620832—dc23       2015004338

Henry Holt books may be purchased for business or promotional use. For information on bulk purchases,
please contact the Macmillan Corporate and Premium Sales Department at (800) 221-7945 x5442
or by e-mail at specialmarkets@macmillan.com.

First Edition—2016 / Designed by Arree Chung and April Ward
The artist used acrylic paint on Rives BFK paper, found paper,
and Adobe Photoshop to create the illustrations for this book.

Printed in China by Toppan Leefung Printing Ltd., Dongguan City, Guangdong Province

1  3  5  7  9  10  8  6  4  2

# GETTING STARTED

**M**any parents find potty training frustrating, with false alarms and the inevitable accident. The truth is that all children, left to their own devices, will become potty trained eventually, especially when they become physically aware of how uncomfortable a wet diaper is and, of course, when they realize that Mommy, Daddy, and Big Brother or Sister use the potty!

When my wife and I started to potty train our son, Abe, we invented a method called free style. Abe would make up styles for using the potty, and we would try to guess what they were. Instead of worrying about when he would be ready or how long the process would take, we decided to have fun with it. The result was a lesson and a game that kept the whole family laughing and inspired a book—*How to Pee: Potty Training for Boys.*

Many of Abe's styles included props—masks, swords, lightsabers, hats—and we encouraged him to be as wacky as possible. He liked to pee outside, so we designated a few areas where he could do this in our garden. Of course, we also found ways to bring the game inside to the toilet. Abe was quickly potty trained, and even a year later, he would come up with a new style, using his creativity—and keeping our bathrooms clean.

This same method is just as fun and successful for girls. When our daughter, Noa, came along, we felt much better prepared and excited to share her older brother's method with her. We loved seeing how she made it her own, using magic wands, fairy wings, tiaras, and wigs as props.

I hope this book will spark your imagination (and keep you laughing) while you and your girl follow the simple steps to mastering the art of potty training.

—Dr. Todd

STEP 4 Sit upon your throne.

# Fresh-Air Style

STEP 1

Stroll into
the garden.

Water the plants.

# Witchy Style

**STEP 1** Grab a broom.

**STEP 2** Put on your pointy hat.

**STEP 3**

Raise your
magic wand.

# DANCI-PARTY STYLE

**STEP 1**

Put on the tunes.

Turn on the
disco lights.

STEP 3

Wave your glow sticks.

STEP 4

Shake your booty and get down!

# Tea Party Style

STEP ①

Send the invitations.

You're Invited to a party

STEP **2** Set out your finest china.

STEP **3** Pour the tea.

# Royal Ball Style

**STEP 1**

Hang the streamers.

STEP **2** Find a fancy dress.

STEP **3** Don your feather boa.

STEP **4** Waltz your way to the toilet.

# Fairy Style

STEP 1

Adjust your wings.

STEP 2 Prepare for takeoff.

STEP 3 Fly to the bathroom.

Sprinkle your
fairy dust.

# Ballerina Style

STEP

**Point your toes.**

**STEP 2**
Take tiny steps.

**STEP 3**
Twirl.

**STEP 4**
Bend your knees over the potty.

# LITTLE STAR STYLE

STEP 1

Watch the sky turn to night.

# GYMNAST STYLE

STEP **1** Get a running start.

STEP
**2** Mount.

STEP
**3**

Release.

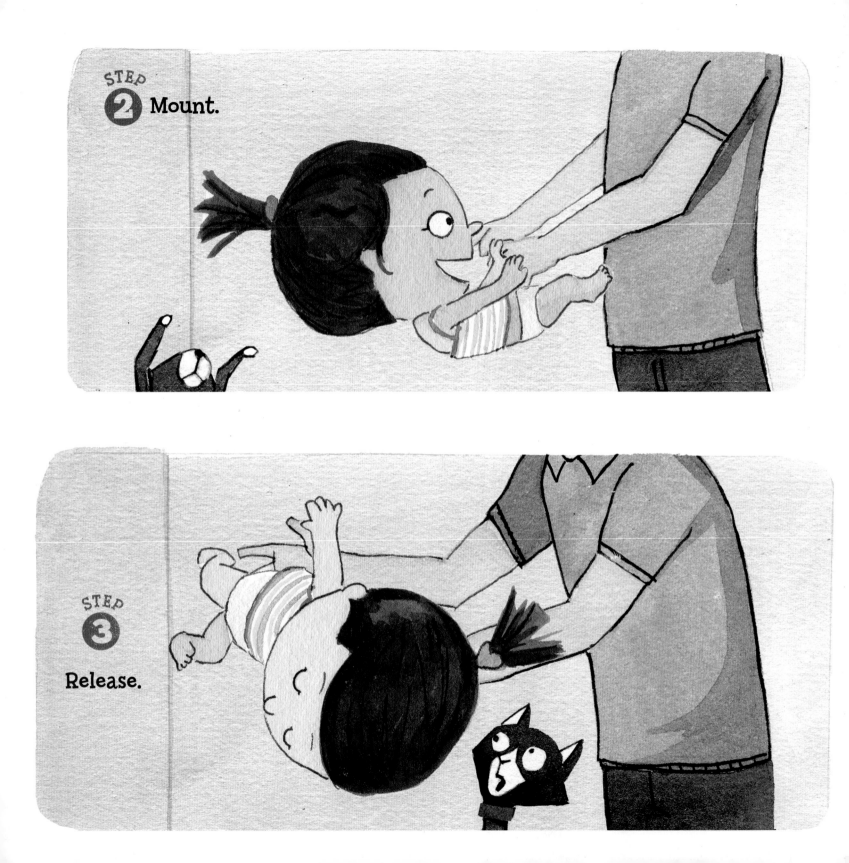

STEP 4

Stick the landing.

# A NOTE TO PARENTS

As a Family Practice physician, I'm always looking for ways to explain to parents that being potty trained is a normal developmental milestone. One of the first things I tell anxious parents is that I see a lot of kids who are not potty trained at age three, but I almost never see four-year-olds in diapers. This usually helps parents relax and buys a little more time for the child to figure it out on her own. In addition, girls seem to be able to potty train (control their sphincters) slightly earlier than boys do, so don't be surprised if your daughter wants to use the potty earlier than your son did.

Today, much of the pressure to potty train early comes from preschools and day cares that insist children are out of diapers before they are admitted. But many two-year-olds are not developmentally ready to potty train. That said, I believe that learning not to wet yourself is a very basic human instinct and children are aware of this as early as eighteen to thirty-six months old. Unfortunately, because modern diapers are so sturdy and comfortable, children are barely aware when they are wet, so they can't respond to the stimulus and learn how to stay clean. I'm not saying using diapers on your child will do her harm; it just might delay this milestone.

I often tell parents that when children start to ask for a new diaper or mention that they are peeing, they are ready to be potty trained. A training potty should be your first investment. Buy a small, simple one and place it next to your toilet. Your child will see you using the potty and, like in other things, will model her behavior on yours. At first, she may sit on the potty while still wearing a diaper. Do not worry: she is well on her way to figuring it out on her own.

Another tip I give parents is to get rid of the diaper. Let your child run around naked for a few hours at a time. Eventually, she will figure it out. There might be a few accidents, but soon enough, she'll remember what she's seen you do and make her way to the potty to do her business.

# A FEW BASIC RULES

 **1** Don't pressure your child. Remember, this is a natural process.

**2** Don't punish your child for having accidents.

 **3** Don't worry if your child is not potty trained even if it seems as if all the other three-year-olds you know are.

**4** Don't worry about a few accidents on your floor.

**5** If your child says she has to pee and she isn't near a potty, don't rush her to the toilet. Let her hold it for a moment as you go calmly to the bathroom. If she has an accident, see rule 4.

**6** If your child regresses and starts to have accidents again, it's okay to use a training diaper. It's best if you have your child put it on like underwear.

**7** If your child continues to have accidents and it is causing stress for your family, see rule 1. Don't be afraid to go back to diapers for a while and try potty training again in a few weeks. But make sure your daughter has a few hours a day without a diaper on to get used to the sensation.

# GOOD LUCK!